a smart girl's g understanding her family

feelings, fighting & figuring it out

by Amy Lynch
illustrated by Lauren Scheuer

⭐ American Girl®

Published by American Girl Publishing, Inc.
Copyright © 2007, 2009 by American Girl, LLC

Questions or comments? Call 1-800-845-0005,
visit our Web site at **americangirl.com**, or write to Customer Service,
American Girl, 8400 Fairway Place, Middleton, WI 53562.

Printed in China   *5203 2538* *2/13*
11 12 13 14 15 LEO 10 9 8 7 6 5 4

Editorial Development: Therese Kauchak Maring, Michelle Nowadly Watkins
Art Direction and Design: Chris Lorette David
Production: Sarah Boecher, Jeannette Bailey, Judith Lary
Illustrations: Lauren Scheuer

This book is not intended to replace the advice of psychologists or other health-care professionals. It should be considered an additional resource only. Questions and concerns about mental health should always be discussed with a health-care provider.

Amy Lynch is a writer and speaker specializing in communication between girls, young adults, and their families. She contributed to *Raising an American Girl: Parenting Advice for the Real World* and is the author of *"How Can You Say That?": What to Say to Your Daughter When One of You Just Said Something Awful*, both from American Girl Publishing. She consults about young people in the workplace through her company, Bottom Line Conversations.

Dear Reader,

This book is about you and the people you are closest to—your family. They're the sisters or brothers who bug you sometimes but who are there for you when you're in a tight spot. They're the parents who wake you in the morning and give you a hug at night. They're the people who live with you and love you, who may embarrass you once in a while, but who believe in you more than anyone else on earth.

In this book you'll find ideas and activities to help you understand your family, create memories with them, and negotiate solutions when you disagree.

Your family—with both its precious moments and its prickly ones—is **your family.** When all is said and done, they can't do without the ideas, the laughter, the tears, and the love that come from **you.** You are the girl who makes your family complete.

Your friends at American Girl

contents

family first aid . . . 26

get close . . . and closer! . . . 52

family fun coupons and awards

your family

Who tucked you in at night when you were little? Who remembers the first time you rode your bike or hit a softball? Your family.

Your family is still here for you. And that's great—because it's easier to take the changes life is throwing your way when you're surrounded by people who love you. The secret is learning to understand your family and the changes they are going through, too.

family basics

There's no magic recipe for a family. Families can be made up of all kinds of ingredients. And when those ingredients are mixed together, each family comes out in its own unique way.

The family in your life today might be like this:

my family recipe
///
- two sets of grandparents
- two parents
- my brother
- my dog, Frank

or this:

my family recipe
- my grandmother
- my parents
- my stepmom
- my brother and stepsister
- my new baby half brother

You may live with your family all in one home, or you may split your time between your parents' homes. It doesn't matter—you're all still FAMILY.

*A *stepsibling* is the child of your stepparent from a different relationship. A *half sibling* shares one of your parents.

List the names of your family members here, and write
one positive trait that you like about each person.

Name: _____

Something I like about this person: _____

_____

Name: _____

Something I like about this person: _____

_____

Name: _____

Something I like about this person: _____

_____

Name: _____

Something I like about this person: _____

_____

Name: _____

Something I like about this person: _____

_____

Name: _____

Something I like about this person: _____

_____

Pretend you happen to overhear your mother or father on the phone describing you to someone you've never met. What would she or he say? Don't think about this too hard—just jot down three or four words.

_____

_____

_____

_____

What are some good words your brother or sister would use to describe you?

_____

_____

_____

_____

When you were younger, you would have listed *different* words from those you just wrote to describe yourself. Look at the words on your lists. Put an X next to words that are different from what you would have written a year ago. Those words show *you're changing*.

BIG truth

You *are* changing.

In fact, between the ages of 8 and 12, you change more quickly than anybody else in your family, unless there's a baby crawling around your house.

When you were a baby, you went from crawling to walking in only a few months. Now, for the second time in your life, your brain and body change so fast that you may feel, think, and act very differently in only weeks.

looking back

How have you changed during the past year? Maybe you joined a team or a club, discovered you like to speak French, or learned to boogie board.

In horseback riding I can canter and jump now. Those things took courage to learn.
Courtney, age 11

I moved last year and that changed me. Now I know I can deal with new things, even if at first I don't like them.
Katie, age 10

I'm at a much more advanced reading level than I was last year, and I learned to do a back walkover.
Liana, age 9

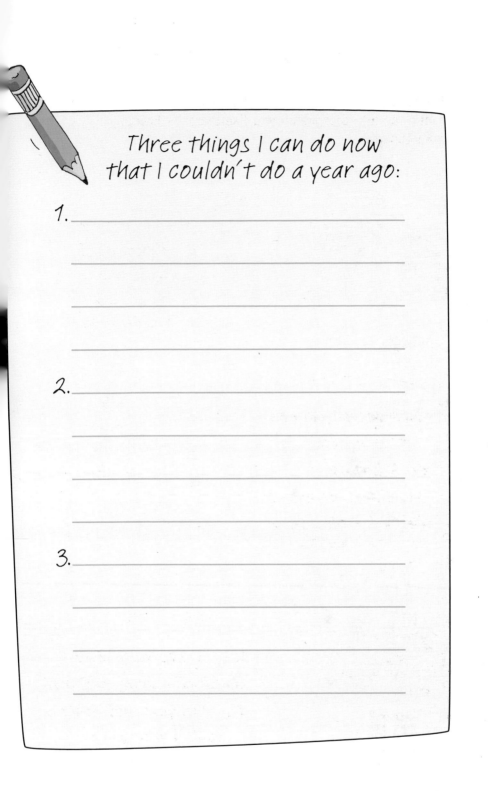

Three things I can do now
that I couldn't do a year ago:

1. _____

_____

_____

_____

2. _____

_____

_____

_____

3. _____

_____

_____

_____

green light?

By now you understand that you are changing, and fast—so fast that you're like a traffic light stuck on green for go.

This is exciting for you! But your mom or dad may act like a yellow light or even a red one, signaling for you to slow down or even stop.

More than anything, your parents want to keep you safe. If you want to ride your bike to the store or go to a movie with your friends, you may think, *Fun!* But your parents may say, "I don't know about this." Then again, they may say, "Go for it!"

No matter which signal your parents give you, nothing seems the same as it was last year—or maybe even last week.

Every time *you* change, your family changes in some way, too. See if these examples fit your family:

• You understand jokes now, so your parents tell you more jokes.

• You are stronger, so your big sister or brother plays basketball against you more seriously.

• You are more responsible, so your family depends on you more.

• You are better at making decisions and taking care of yourself, so your parents let you make more choices.

With everybody changing and everybody busy, how will you find ways to talk about everything you need to discuss? You may wonder . . .

• where to begin if you have questions about body stuff.

• what words to use if you are sad or mad or lonely.

• how to negotiate for more independence.

Don't worry. Your voice is a terrific tool. You can use it, along with your natural savvy, to talk through sticky situations.

communicate!

You're changing, and that's not always easy. Sometimes changes are hard to deal with and to talk about. But, as you may have noticed, slamming doors and feeling embarrassed doesn't get you anywhere.

Now is the time to learn to communicate better with your family—to keep your minds and hearts open so that you can talk things out.

)... could you PLEASE KNOCK Before y

KE it When you and I Sit and chat abo

anna Asked me about what he said, AND when

LLY DiSSed me, but I didnt want to look li

Teacher. She couldNt Just Tell Her, so

Really Miss my friend Danielle. Why

hil Said he didn't really Mean it that W

= BEEN FEELing Kind Of SAd ABou

yelled At you. I Should have THough

RACE AND Sarah to THE movies oN

THOught I WAS HER BEst FRIend,

out it WHEN I KNOW she didnt m

go to THE MALL oN SATURDA

RTY, BUT micaela Said she could

ave a pRoject due oN THURSdAy so I TH

iNd of SNOOTY LATELY, BUT She didnt

s house A   School oN

you PICK   at her house A

PRACTICE iN   pouring RaiN! a

nk She Should ApOLogize TO ME becau

17

little things that say a lot

A loving message is like a cozy blanket or a bowl of hot oatmeal on a winter morning. It warms you all the way through. And you can send warm messages any time you want. Check out the ideas below, and let your family know you're there to care.

Share YOURSELF. Your parents miss you if you don't spend time with them. Surprise them! Take time now and then to hang out with them. Play a game, take a walk, or bake a cake—together.

Be sympathetic. When your dad is sick and your sister gets cut from the team, they'll need you to be there for them 100 percent. Let the feelings flow. Your family will feel better just knowing that you care.

Meet and greet. "Have a great day" and "welcome home" can be real pick-me-ups for the person walking through the door. These may be the best words your mom will hear all day, especially since they come from you.

Give healthy hugs. Did you know that hugs can make us healthier? People who get plenty of hugs tend to get sick less often than those who don't. So share hugs with your family and spread the good feeling around. Remember, you always have the right to say NO to hugs and cuddles if you don't want them.

Say "please" and "thanks." Little things count, and these little words really work. No wonder some people call them magic!

Stay in touch. When your parents travel away from home, send an e-mail or a letter to let them know you miss them. The trip will seem shorter to them and the distance closer when they feel your love.

Schedule it. Dance lessons, scouts, soccer practice, babysitting, and overnights—you have a million places to go. Put your schedule on the family calendar ahead of time. Be part of the plan.

how to talk to your parents about anything

Of course, not every problem can be solved by being kinder, gentler, and more considerate to the people in your family.

Some problems are bigger than that. Sometimes you need advice. Or something big has happened and when it comes to talking to Mom or Dad about it, you don't have a clue how to start.

Maybe you're shy when it comes to talking about something personal. Or maybe this problem is **so big** that you honestly don't know where to begin. Or maybe you're worried about how your parent will react. No matter what, these techniques can help.

Begin by **picking the right time.** You need your parent's full attention in order to have a good talk. Try not to bring up something when it's past your bedtime or when your parent is in a rush. If it's hard to get a parent alone, make an "appointment." Your parents want to know what's on your mind, so ask them to make time for you.

Instead of this:

Try this:

Go slowly. What you need to say probably isn't simple, so don't try to get it all out in one breath. Give your parents the details they need to make a decision before you start trying to bargain with them. Remember that conversation is about give-and-take. Listen to your parents, and they'll listen to you.

Instead of this:

Try this:

Be honest. Your parents will respond better if they believe that you're telling the whole truth and not trying to avoid blame. Take responsibility for your part in getting into trouble or earning a bad grade. If you've done something wrong, 'fess up. Things get worse the longer you wait.

Instead of this:

BUT IT WASN'T MY FAULT!

Try this:

I'm sorry this happened. I've been afraid to tell you about it, but I want to try to fix things.

Try, try again. When you fly off the handle, your parents have a hard time seeing your point of view. If you're angry or frustrated, take a break from the conversation. Excuse yourself, and go somewhere to cool off. Gather your thoughts, and when you're ready, try talking to your parents again.

Instead of this:

You don't get it! You treat me like a baby!

Try this:

This means a lot to me. I want you to understand.

22

Be brave. You might carry around a question or confession for a long time before you get up the nerve to let it out. But your parents almost always can help you solve a problem or answer a big question, and you'll almost always feel better afterward. Talk to your parents. You'll be glad you did.

Instead of this:

Try this:

help!

All kinds of girls write to *American Girl* magazine for help on communicating with their moms and dads.

My parents think I need to be perfect. If I get a B instead of an A, they make a big fuss over it. It's important to get good grades, but they're overdoing it.
—Not Perfect

Parents can't help it: they want the best for their kids, and that's what makes them push. They also may focus on grades when what they really want is just to be sure you're trying your hardest. Still, most parents also know it isn't possible to be best at everything. Talk with your mom and dad, and ask if together you can choose the subjects in which it's crucial for you to shine. They may be more accepting of your grades if they're sure you're reaching for the stars when it counts.

If my mom is having a stressful day, she can be really cranky. I hate to be around her when she's like that. Help me!
—Don't Know What to Do

When Mom has had a hard day, the best thing you can do is give her some peace and quiet. Hang out in your room and read a book. If you have siblings, invite them to play a quiet board game with you so that they stay out of Mom's hair, too. You might even want to write a little note telling your mom how much you love her and leave it where she'll find it. These things might not seem like much, but they will be just what she needs to feel better.

My dad is really critical of me in sports. I try to do my best, but it seems like it's never enough for him. He even says rude things about my coaches.
—Discouraged and Upset

Your dad wants you to do your best. That's good. But he may have forgotten that sports should also be fun. See if you can remind him. Tell him that when he's upset with the coach or with you, the fun disappears. Let him know that cheering helps you more than criticism. Be prepared: in the heat of a game, your dad may forget to keep his cool. If so, your best defense is to stay focused on the game and your teammates—not on those shouts you hear from the sidelines.

I am a sixth-grader who got my first detention today. I feel like I'm losing my perfect reputation. I want my image and my parents' trust back.
—No Longer Perfect

It sounds as if you made a mistake. Here's a little secret—everyone does. No one is perfect, so don't be unfair to yourself by expecting to be. In time, if you show that you've learned from your mistake by not repeating it, you'll regain your parents' trust. In fact, your parents will probably forgive you more easily than you will forgive yourself. Tell them how you feel. Then serve your detention, and move on!

family first aid

Do your part to prevent misunderstandings. When trouble happens (and it will!), learn to help clear the air.

BIG truth

Families fight. It's normal.

Your family members will not get along perfectly all the time, unless they are one of the following:

a. mannequins

b. robots

c. fairy-tale characters

If your family is made up of real live humans, then family feelings *will* get out of control from time to time—even though you love one another with all your hearts. So what should you do when things get rough? Learn to help solve problems. If you do that, it'll be a sure sign you're growing up.

parent spotlight

Because your parents are always there, it can be easy to overlook that they are changing, too.

The truth is that parents and stepparents can't stop changing any more than you can! And the ways they change can affect your life big-time. On the one hand, if your dad starts playing volleyball, he may go to practice on Tuesday evenings instead of staying home with you to watch *Revenge of the Sharks* on the Science Channel. On the other hand, if your mom has started making scrapbooks in her spare time, she may be more available for talks and tea in the afternoon.

Explore the ways your parents or stepparents are changing by putting a check beside the things that are true.

One of my parents or stepparents . . .

☐ has found a new hobby or sport.

☐ has taken a different job.

☐ has divorced or remarried.

☐ exercises more than he or she used to.

☐ exercises less than he or she used to.

☐ has had a parent who was ill or who recently died.

☐ is planning a vacation.

☐ laughs more these days.

☐ acts more serious these days.

☐ recently celebrated a big anniversary or birthday.

Do you ever get wound up and anxious thinking about your day, your homework, or problems you have with friends? That's natural.

We all get stuck in thoughts about ourselves sometimes, but when we do, it can cause family conflict . . . especially with your parents. If you forget to think about their point of view—the chores they need you to help with, the times they need you to get home, the pressures they feel to get their work done—you can get in a jam with them before you know it!

Don't stay cooped up inside your own head. Sure, it's interesting in there. But once in a while, give this mind-reading exercise a try:

1. Pick a parent.

2. Now, use your imagination. What does she or he think:
   - first thing in the morning?
   - when waiting at a stop sign?
   - just before drifting off to sleep?

3. When you have a minute, ask your parent and find out the real answers.

See, wasn't that interesting?

stop the fight before it starts

Sometimes the people closest to our hearts are the ones we take for granted the most—and that can lead to hurt feelings and fights. Here are some ways to show your family that they matter to you.

Start the day gently. Are you half asleep in the a.m.? You're not alone. Give everybody in your family a little extra understanding in the morning. They're sleepwalking just like you!

Lend a hand. Did you know that parents do nine or ten chores for every one chore a kid does? So clear the table, scrape the scraps, and toss the trash. Doing chores without being asked? Bonus points!

My dog is like family. I remember washing him when he was a puppy. I took him in the shower and then wrapped him in a towel. It makes me feel good to help out around the house. I know my mom depends on me.
—Hannah, age 10

Notice your noise. Music is great! But don't play it too loud. Use headphones or turn down the volume when your brother is doing his homework or your mom is taking a nap. It's better for your eardrums, too.

Try to do your homework early. The closer it is to bedtime, the harder it is to get the work done, and the harder it is for your parents to help.

Stash your stuff. Keeping your things in your room helps the family stay on the go. And nobody will trip over your backpack in the hallway.

Beat a retreat. Feeling moody? Try not to take it out on your family. When even *you* know you're crabby, do something that helps you feel soothed, like playing with your pet, taking a warm bath, or reading a good book.

Not now, but later. When you ask someone in the family for help or for a favor, try asking for it *later* instead of right this minute. Then the answer is more likely to be "yes."

Joke gently. Some people in your family probably can make a joke and take a joke, but not everyone can. And even those who *can* can't take jokes all the time. Respect the feelings family members have about teasing and tickling. They'll be more likely to respect your feelings, too.

BIG truth

You have more power than you think
to affect the peace in your family.

Use it.

your reaction style

When there is conflict at home, how do you react? Think about the last time you got into an argument with a member of your family. Below, choose the kind of "geography" that best describes the way you reacted to the situation.

☐ **Volcano**: You exploded with a flash of flame. Then your anger went away pretty quickly.

☐ **Iceberg**: You didn't go on the attack, but you had lots of angry feelings underneath the surface. Those feelings lasted a long time after the fight was done.

☐ **Rock**: During the argument, your thoughts and reactions slowed down and felt heavy, like boulders. It was hard to find the words you wanted.

☐ **River**: Your mind was working at top speed. You thought of lots of ways to make others see things your way, and the words came easily to you.

Each reaction style has the power to do harm. A *volcano* makes everybody cower. An *iceberg* remembers hurts. A *rock* resists solutions, and a *river* is determined to make other people agree with her.

Now, here's the best part. You can use the power of your reaction style for making up!

Volcanos: Your flash of flaming anger may have inflicted more hurt than you realize, and there's nothing like a sincere apology for making things right. In fact, apologize twice. Over time you'll learn to cool the flames with people you love.

Icebergs: Wait a day before you make your next move. Then check in with the family member who argued with you. Tell him or her that you are trying to let go of hard feelings. Apologize for holding on to your hurt. Offer a hug if you are ready, and feel the world of love inside the hug that you get.

Rocks: People may think you aren't upset by the fight or that you don't care about their hurt feelings. No matter what your part was in the argument, be sure to tell the other person that you know she is upset and that you care about how she feels. Then she'll know how strong and true your heart is!

Rivers: Remember that there is no "right" in a fight. You may win the argument but leave lots of hard feelings behind. Next time, do something radical—practice losing! That's right; let somebody else have the last word and see what happens. Peace can return more quickly that way, and you can save your River Power for showing others how much you care.

Volcanos, icebergs, rocks, and *rivers* all: No matter what your style is, you have some control over how you react. The next time the room heats up with an argument, think about being a *lake*—cool, calm, and deep.

alike or different?

Figuring out how you are similar to—and different from—the people in your family can help you understand them . . . and understand how to get along with them. Maybe *you* have a quick temper, but your sister hardly ever gets upset. Maybe you and your mother both laugh when you're nervous. Think about it!

Ready for a challenge? On the next two pages, write down the names of three people in your family.

Get set. Find a timer and set it for three minutes. During those three minutes, you're going to think of all the ways you are similar to and different from the people you chose. You don't need to write full sentences. Just write enough to make the idea clear. You can write about physical attributes (you both have green eyes), artistic tastes (neither of you like opera), or emotional things (you both cry at movies or yell when you're mad).

Go! Start the timer.

Tick

Tick

Tick

tick

Name: _____

How we're alike: _____

_____

_____

How we're different: _____

_____

_____

Name: _____

How we're alike: _____

_____

_____

How we're different: _____

_____

_____

Name: _____

How we're alike: _____

_____

_____

How we're different: _____

_____

_____

When three minutes are up, stop and count your answers. Whose "alike list" is the longest? Whose "different list" is the longest?

The person most like you may be the one you get along with best. The person most different from you may be someone you have trouble understanding sometimes. Getting along with that person may require patience and your very best negotiating skills. Either way, you can learn from your lists!

word power

Words are powerful things, whether you're working things out with a parent, stepparent, brother, sister, stepsibling, or naughty dog. Say the words below out loud. Pause after each word to notice how it makes your body feel.

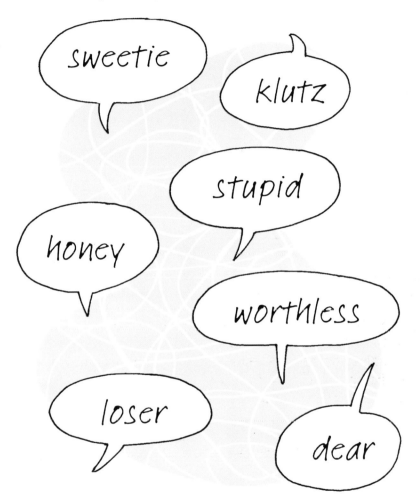

Chances are, saying these words made you feel something. The kinder words—sweetie, dear, and honey—may have given you a little smile inside or made you feel positive. The unkind words—klutz, stupid, worthless, and loser—may have made you utter a mental "ouch."

Just as *these* words made you feel good or bad, the words *you* use affect the emotions of everyone in your family. When you say loving words or fighting ones, the "emotional temperature" at your house changes instantly!

41

translation, please

Angry words often mean more than one thing and can stem from more than one feeling. The words below are good examples. Draw lines from the words on the left to their most likely meanings on the right. Then look at the red words to see what feelings might cause someone to burst out with these phrases.

Words

1. You're not the boss of me!

2. You lied to me!

3. Shut up!

4. You're stupid!

Meanings

a. Something changed, and I don't like it!

CONFUSED
DISAPPOINTED

b. I can't deal with this right now. Leave me alone.

STRESSED OUT

c. I feel so bad about myself that I have to tell you you're no good, too.

ASHAMED
AFRAID

d. I'm not in control.

HELPLESS
POWERLESS

The answers are on the next page.

BIG truth

Mean words are never O.K., and there is no excuse for anyone to be cruel to you. But if you understand that lots of different feelings may cause someone to use angry words, it may help you figure out what's going on. And *that* makes it easier to talk with someone when you're trying to work things out.

ANSWERS: 1 matches best with d, 2 matches best with a, 3 matches best with b, and 4 matches best with c.

43

neutral words

If you find yourself in a disagreement, using neutral words can be like robbing a fire of oxygen. It makes the fire go out! The next time you're in a heated argument, try using some of these peace-making phrases. They don't mean that you agree or give in, but they can slow down the pace of the squabble and lower the boiling point.

talking it out

Try these conversation starters when you want to come to an understanding with someone.

I'm ready to make peace. Are you?

I don't like it when we fight.

I feel sad that we argued. Can we try that again?

Read body language. You may not need to say anything to get a conversation rolling. Look into the other person's eyes. If you see love there, you can offer a hug. Chances are, that will naturally get the talk flowing!

Brainstorm. Ask the other person to brainstorm with you about some ways you can avoid having the same quarrel again. Two brains are better than one—at least, they are when they're not in an argument!

I have a sister who is five years old. If we get into a fight and I want to make up, I offer to play with her. She loves that.
—Skylar, age 10

let's make a deal

You may not realize that you already know how to *negotiate,* or help find a solution that works for everyone involved in a disagreement. But you do. Whether you're the oldest child, an only child, the youngest in the family, or anywhere in between, you work out agreements with family members all the time.

Think about the past few days. What deals did you make with people in your family? Did everybody get what he or she wanted? Did you have any arguments that could have been solved through negotiation? List a few of each here.

Deals I made:

_____

_____

_____

_____

_____

Arguments that could have been deals:

_____

_____

_____

_____

_____

chilling out

Have you ever noticed how bad your body feels after an argument? Disagreements are hard on everyone! Being in a fight robs you of energy, peace, and well-being. SO, take care of yourself. Try the following ideas for chilling out when family fever runs high.

Just breathe. Deep breathing will soothe and steady you. If someone says something that gets you riled, before you say anything back, take two

l . . o . . n . . g,

s . . l . . o . . w

breaths. This alone can take the wind out of an argument.

Understand that you're "mad all over." Getting angry affects more than your heart and your head. Your whole body feels it! When you're angry, your heart beats faster, your muscles tense, your breathing speeds up, and your brain produces "angry" chemicals. It can take at least 20 minutes for all of that to go away. Until then, some part of your body is still mad! Give yourself time to calm down and work through your emotions.

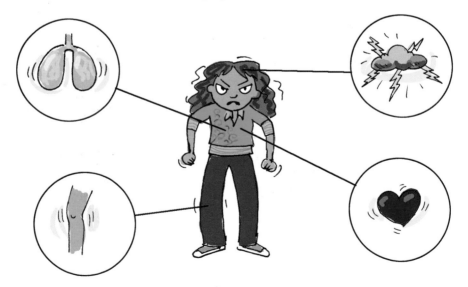

Calm down by getting physical. Can't stop an argument? Say, "You know, I'm feeling _____," and fill in the emotion you feel. Then explain: "I need time to calm down." Leave the scene, and get moving! Shoot hoops hard, take a fast run, jump into a pool, jump on your bike, or climb a tree. Use your muscles to calm your mind.

Ask questions. When you feel calmer, ask yourself some questions about what happened. This gets the thinking part of your brain working rather than the feelings part. Writing your answers in your diary may help you think more clearly.

Have some gumption. If you argue with someone you love, odds are you'll feel pretty awful about it. But part of living in a family is learning to stand up for yourself. If you have *gumption,* it means you're willing to take a step, be bold, or—in this case— speak up. If your brother teases you too harshly, say so. If you got blamed for something that you didn't do, say so.

You don't have to yell to do this. You just have to keep saying how you feel and what you need until somebody hears you! If things get tense, be patient and keep talking. This is what it means to stand on your own two feet.

your personal first-aid kit

Some families have quiet disagreements; others have big, loud clashes. Big or little, family conflicts can make our hearts hurt. Put a check mark next to the ideas you can use to take care of yourself when there is tension in your family. Add your own ideas in the blank spaces.

I can . . .

☐ remind myself that even when we argue, we still love one another.

☐ cry and let my feelings out.

☐ ask for a comforting hug.

☐ move my body and get physical.

☐ talk to a good friend about my feelings.

☐ ask for help from a loving adult.

☐ write or draw how I feel.

☐ get outside and soak up some nature.

☐ _____

☐ _____

☐ _____

saying "sorry"

If you did something that hurt someone's feelings, come clean! Apologizing will help you—and the other person—feel better, and then you can start fresh.

Keep the apology short and simple. Just say you're sorry for what you did or said. Resist the urge to make excuses or explain *why* you did what you did. That way, the apology won't be about YOU but about the person who was hurt.

About that lump in your throat: Sometimes apologizing can be embarrassing, even painful. If you need courage, give yourself a little time—but don't avoid apologizing.

get close . . . and closer!

The secret to getting closer to your family is being curious about their stories, their dreams, and their hearts. Have fun together! Here are some activities you can do that will make you smile—and help you get to know one another even better.

get the scoop

Think you know your family well? Complete the sentences below by circling a family member and filling in the blank. Next, become a reporter. Interview your family members to see how many of the questions you answered right.

1. One of my mom's/dad's favorite books is

_____ .

2. My sister's/brother's favorite room in our house is

_____ .

3. One of my mom's/dad's favorite movies is

_____ .

4. When my grandmother/grandfather was a child, she/he

lived in _____ .

5. When my other grandmother/grandfather was a child,

she/he lived in _____ .

6. At my age, my mom/dad wanted to be a

_____ when she/he grew up.

7. If my brother/sister could travel anywhere in the world, it

would be _____ .

8. One of the biggest adventures my mom/dad ever had was

_____ .

9. One of my mom's/dad's closest friends is named

_____ .

10. My sister's/brother's best part of the day is

_____ .

11. My mom's/dad's favorite kind of music is

_____ .

Scoring

9 or more correct

Congratulations! You already listen closely to the people in your family. If you were the contestant on a family quiz show, you could win first prize!

5–8 correct

You've been doing a good job paying attention to details in your family. With a little work, you could write an encyclopedia of family trivia.

4 or fewer correct

There's a whole world of fun family facts out there to discover. The more you know about your family members, the better you'll understand them—and that can mean more closeness and good times at home.

Celebrate your specialness! Every family member has quirks. Strange as it sounds, those are things that can make families closer.

My dad is a terrible singer. When he sings, my sister and I start singing as loud as we can so we can't hear him, but then he sings louder. Then my mom starts yelling at us all to be quiet. The weird thing is we do this every day!
Madeline, age 11

Our dog, Rusty, makes this barky sound, and my mom talks back to him. Then he talks back to her. They even talk about the weather!
Annie, age 10

My mom gets excited over nothing. Today she started dancing because she got a book about flowers. It was crazy.
Kellye, age 12

My aunt always says, "Cute, cute, cute!" when she likes something. She says it three times, never once or twice—always three.
Rhonda, age 11

Enjoy the nighttime neighborhood. If you live in a place where you can walk at night, ask your family to take an evening stroll. The world feels totally different in the dark, and there's a special closeness that comes from seeing your street at bedtime. Besides, a walk in the evening is a good time for sharing stories of the day or memories from the past. Don't forget a flashlight!

Share your dreams. When you wake up, tell the story of your dream to your parent or sister quickly, before you forget. Does anybody in your family have ideas about what your dream might mean? Are there clues in the dream that can help you solve a daytime prob-lem? If morning is too busy, write down your dream and share it in the evening. Ask your family what they dreamed about, too!

Join family members while they do something they love. Watch hockey with your brother, or listen to jazz with your mom. Bake bread or hit golf balls with your dad. Even if it's not your favorite thing to do, it will draw you closer. Maybe next time, they'll do what you love to do—with you!

Plant memories. Plant a tree or a bush together to mark a family event. Graduating from elementary school? That's a big event. Anniversaries and birthdays are, too. So are sad times such as losing a grandparent. Your family will feel connected on the day you plant the tree and every time you see it all year round.

Play "Best Thing, Worst Thing." At the dinner table, ask each person to tell the best thing that happened that day. Then ask each person to tell the worst part of his or her day. If people are in a joking mood, have a contest to see who had the very best and very worst days. If your family is feeling serious, simply share your stories. Either way, you'll feel closer than you did before!

Play by the numbers. Grab any family member, or divide your family into two teams. Write the list below on another sheet of paper so that you have two copies. Yell "One, two, three—go!" and see which team can find the answers most quickly.

When you're done, see if both teams got the same answers. The team with most correct answers gets to take the other team out for ice cream!

Number of jars of peanut butter
   in the house _____

Number of windows in the house _____

Number of pets in the family _____

Number of telephones the family has
   (count cell phones, too!) _____

Number of shoes in the front closet _____

Number of steps leading up to the front door _____

Number of bicycles in the family _____

Number of drawers in the kitchen _____

Number of rugs in the house
   (count the doormats, too!) _____

Share a read. Have you read a good book recently? Your family might enjoy lots of the books you like, too. Loan a book to your mom, dad, sister, or brother. Talking about exciting plot twists or comparing what you thought about a book can make for great conversations. ("Could you believe the ending?" "What would you have done in her place?" "I cried in that part, too.")

Get game crazy. Talk with your family about regularly setting aside an evening to play games. You could call it Find Family Fun Night! On FFF Night, turn off the computer, TV, and cell phones, and break out a game. Teach a younger sibling how to play something new. Other times, choose a game based on luck so that even little sibs will have a chance to win.

Send signals. Speak your own private language by making up family-only code words or signals. A tug on your ear could mean "Look at that." Saying "FHB" when guests are over for dinner could be code for "family, hold back" so that there will be plenty of food for guests. But be careful about using family signals in public. They can give you incurable giggles!

Once we were at the zoo and couldn't find the bathroom. We also couldn't find the elephants. So now when we say, "Where is the elephant?" it really means something else!
Fran, age 9

If something comes up at dinner that my mom doesn't want me to hear, she says, "Come help me with the dishes." Everybody laughs because we all know what she means!
Victoria, age 10

Make it official. Schools have official songs. States have official birds. Why not your family? Brainstorm with other family members to fill in the blanks below:

Family song: _____

Family mascot: _____

Family food: _____

Family cheer: _____

_____

_____

Family color: _____

Family bird: _____

Draw your family flag here. Include symbols, words, and colors that represent your family to you.

Look into the future. Make a list of things that are true right now about you and your family. You can also make predictions for the coming year. Seal the list in an envelope marked "Open Next Year." Pack it away with the holiday decorations. Read the list together next year to see how things have changed!

Get tangled up in love. Find a ball of yarn or string. Ask your family to stand in a circle. Start by holding the end of the string and tossing the ball to someone else. (It will unwind as you toss it.) After you toss the ball, say something good about the person who caught it.

Next, have the catcher toss the ball to someone else—still holding on to part of the string—and say what he or she appreciates about that person. Keep tossing the ball around the circle until the string is all unwound. What a web of good feelings you made!

Cheer for the home team. What are the biggest challenges your family members are going through? Is your brother having a hard time with math? Has your mom been spending long hours at the office? Leave a note cheering him or her on. If you have time, make a banner or a sign using bright, energizing colors. Knowing that you believe in them will help your family members face their troubles and reach their goals.

Here are some other American Girl books you might like:

❏ *I read it.*

❏ *I read it.*

❏ *I read it.*

❏ *I read it.*

❏ *I read it.*

❏ *I read it.*

family fun coupons and awards

Use these handy pullouts to show your family you appreciate them, when you need help apologizing, or when you just want to say thanks.

family award

This award goes to

_____

for being by far the most stupendous and wonderful

_____

in the family, in the whole world and, possibly, in the entire universe.

From: _____

family award

This award goes to

_____

for being by far the most stupendous and wonderful

_____

in the family, in the whole world and, possibly, in the entire universe.

From: _____

Official "I'm Sorry" Certificate
from the Department of Apologies and Mended Fences

To: _____

I am certifiably sorry for what I did. I know it made you feel

☐ sad

☐ angry

☐ upset

☐ all of the above

I care about you very much. Please accept my apology.

From: _____

Official "I'm Sorry" Certificate
from the Department of Apologies and Mended Fences

To: _____

I am certifiably sorry for what I did. I know it made you feel

☐ sad

☐ angry

☐ upset

☐ all of the above

I care about you very much. Please accept my apology.

From: _____

Official "I'm Sorry" Certificate
from the Department of Apologies and Mended Fences

To: _____

I am certifiably sorry for what I did. I know it made you feel

☐ sad

☐ angry

☐ upset

☐ all of the above

I care about you very much. Please accept my apology.

From: _____